JUNIOR FIELD GUIDE

INSECTS
OF
NUNAVUT

WRITTEN BY
Jordan Hoffman

ILLUSTRATED BY
Athena Gubbe

TABLE OF CONTENTS

What Is an Insect? 4

Ground Beetle 8
Mosquito 10
Crane Fly.. 12
Housefly 14
Caribou Warble Fly 16
American Copper Butterfly 18
Brush-Footed Butterfly.................................... 20
Arctic Woolly Bear Moth 22
Northern Bumble Bee 24
Wolf Spider (Arachnid)................................... 26

Glossary 28

What Is an Insect?

Insects are the largest group of animals on Earth. Insects can be found all over Nunavut. You might not notice them because they are usually small or hiding away.

There are many types of insects, and they can be difficult to tell apart. In this field guide, you will learn about some types of insects that you might recognize.

Insects are a group of many different kinds of species that share common qualities. Insects:

- Do not have a backbone
- Have three pairs of jointed legs
- Have one pair of antennae
- Have an **exoskeleton**
- Have a body made of three different parts: the head at the front, the thorax in the middle, and the abdomen at the end

Insects are important for ecosystems because they **pollinate** plants. Some insects also help recycle nutrients in an **ecosystem** by eating dead animals and plants. This helps new plants grow, which produces food for animals that eat plants.

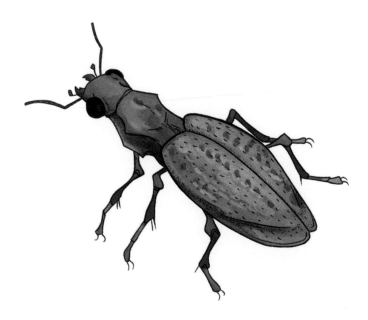

Life Cycle of Insects

Insects go through a process called **metamorphosis.** Metamorphosis means the change from one form to a completely different form. There are two types of metamorphosis: complete metamorphosis and incomplete metamorphosis. All the insects in this book go through complete metamorphosis. The wolf spider, which is not an insect, goes through incomplete metamorphosis.

Insects that experience complete metamorphosis can look and behave like completely different animals from when they are born to when they are adults. Young and adult insects can live in different habitats and even eat different types of food. For example, young butterflies live as **caterpillars** that use their legs to crawl along eating the leaves of plants. Adult butterflies have wings and are able to fly. They eat food such as the **nectar** of flowers.

Here are the steps of complete metamorphosis:

1. The insect starts as an egg.
2. The insect emerges from the egg as a **larva.**
3. The insect enters a period of rest as a **pupa** while transforming from a larva to an adult.
4. The insect emerges from the pupa as an adult.

Here are the steps of incomplete metamorphosis:

1. The insect or arachnid starts as an egg.
2. The insect or **arachnid** emerges from the egg as a nymph or spiderling, which looks like a smaller version of the adult. The nymph or spiderling goes through several periods of **molting,** in which it sheds its exoskeleton and grows a new one. Each time the nymph or spiderling molts it grows slightly larger.
3. The insect or arachnid fully develops into an adult and stops molting. Some insects develop wings as they change from nymphs into adults.

Adaptations of Insects

Most insects live on land and use their legs to walk or dig, or their wings to fly. Some insects can also swim on the surface of the water or under water.

Adaptations are special skills or qualities an insect develops to help it survive in different conditions. For example, in Nunavut, the Arctic woolly bear caterpillar creates chemicals in its body to prevent it from freezing completely in cold temperatures. Other insects, such as mosquitoes, use their wings to fly and search for animals to feed on.

Spiders

Spiders are arachnids. They are not insects, even though they look similar to many insects.

Unlike insects, spiders:

- Have four pairs of legs
- Do not have antennae
- Have two body sections
- Never have wings

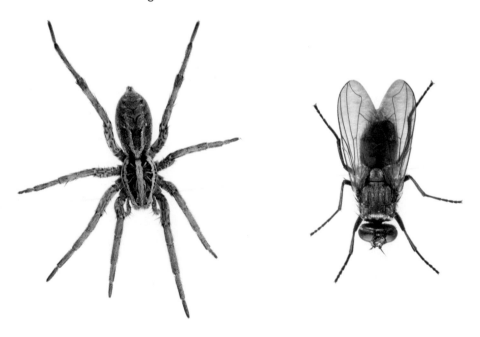

In this guide, you will learn about one species of spider found in the Arctic: the wolf spider.

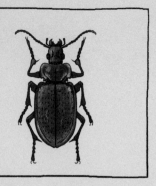

GROUND BEETLE

Appearance

Adult ground beetles are between 0.3 and 6 centimetres long. The bodies of ground beetles are covered in a hard exoskeleton. Ground beetles have narrow heads, with **segmented** antennae and large eyes.

Ground beetles have one pair of wings that has **evolved** to become hardened coverings called elytra. They have one pair of wings hidden underneath their elytra. They also have long, slim legs.

Found all over Nunavut

Range

Most species of ground beetles in Nunavut are found near the treeline or in the Low Arctic. One species is known to occur in the High Arctic. Ground beetles have been identified in Iqaluit, Clyde River, Baker Lake, and Kugluktuk.

Habitat

Ground beetles live on the ground around and under rocks, in cracks in the soil, and near water. They usually hide during the day.

Diet and Feeding

Adult ground beetles are **scavengers** and **predators**. They use their sharp mouthparts to chew food. In Nunavut, they feed on smaller insects, such as the larvae of other species. However, the species found in the High Arctic feeds on flowers. Ground beetles usually feed at night.

The larvae of ground beetles are also predators. They inject juices with their mouths into their prey to help digest it. They can then suck up their food as a liquid.

Life Cycle

Ground beetles experience complete metamorphosis.

1. Ground beetles lay their eggs on the ground or in holes in the soil. Their eggs take around five days to hatch.
2. Once the eggs hatch into larvae, the larvae live in burrows in the soil or under cover on the ground.
3. The larvae pupate under the ground.
4. Adults emerge 5 to 10 days later.

Behaviour

Ground beetles are active at night as they search for food.

Even though ground beetles have wings, they usually don't fly.

Did you know?

Ground beetles can survive the winter as eggs and as adults. They can be found in soil or other protected areas where they are sheltered from the harsh winter conditions.

Mosquito

Found all over Nunavut

Appearance

Adult mosquitoes are between 0.3 and 1.5 centimetres long.

Mosquitoes have small, round heads. The bodies of mosquitoes can be dark grey or black in colour.

Mosquitoes have long, slim antennae and slim, beak-like mouthparts. The mouthparts of female mosquitoes are specialized to suck blood. Only female mosquitoes suck blood.

Mosquitoes have one pair of wings. Their wings are long and narrow, have veins, and are covered in scales.

Range

Mosquitoes can be found all over Nunavut, except for on small islands where there is no **standing water**.

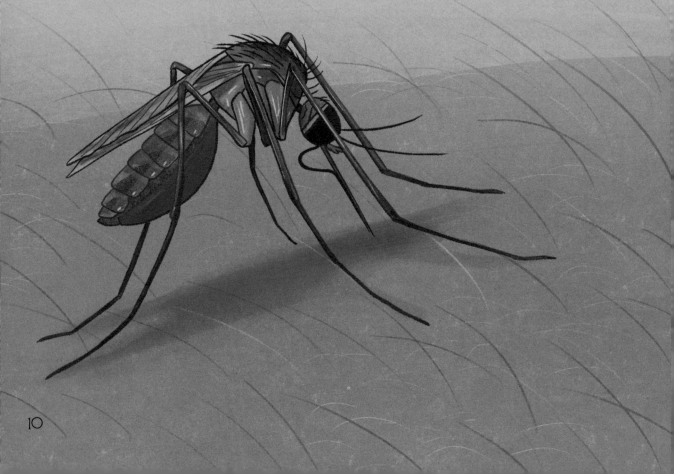

Habitat

Mosquitoes in Nunavut can be found on the tundra. They are usually near areas with standing water, since their larvae and pupae grow in water. These areas include melt pools from ice, puddles, small ponds, and bogs.

You will usually find mosquitoes when it's not very windy, since they have a hard time flying in strong winds.

Diet and Feeding

Female mosquitoes feed on nectar from plants. Females also feed on blood from animals and humans using special needle-like mouthparts. Females use the blood they feed on to help develop their eggs.

In the High Arctic, mosquitoes may not always be able to find animals to feed on for their blood. They have adapted to be able to grow their eggs without this food source.

Male mosquitoes feed on nectar from plants. Sometimes male mosquitoes do not feed at all as adults.

The larvae of mosquitoes feed on **algae** and other small animals in the water, or on material from dead plants. They use brushes around their mouth to collect their food.

Life Cycle

Mosquitoes experience complete metamorphosis.

1. Mosquitoes lay their eggs in standing water near the edges of lakes, in ponds or puddles, or where water is likely to collect from rain or melting snow. The eggs spend the winter frozen in water.
2. In spring, the eggs hatch into larvae called wrigglers. Wrigglers live and feed in the water. They spend two to three weeks as wrigglers.
3. The wrigglers turn into pupae that still live in water and are able to swim.
4. The pupae turn into adults that leave the water and are able to fly.

Behaviour

Female mosquitoes are known to bite many different types of animals, such as caribou, muskoxen, foxes, and even fish! They can be major pests for many species in Nunavut.

In the High Arctic on Ellesmere Island, female mosquitoes' favourite animal to suck blood from is the muskox.

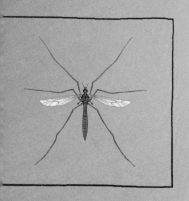

CRANE FLY

Appearance

Have you ever seen what you thought was a giant mosquito? It might have been a crane fly.

Adult crane flies are between 0.8 and 6 centimetres long. Crane flies have long, slim bodies. Their bodies are grey and brown or black in colour.

Crane flies have one pair of wings. Their wings are long. Behind their wings, they have long, stick-like limbs called halteres. The halteres help crane flies balance when they are flying.

Crane flies have short antennae and large eyes on their heads. They also have long and very thin legs.

Found
all over
Nunavut

Range

Crane flies can be found all over Nunavut. There are 4 species in the High Arctic, and there could be up to 40 species in the Low Arctic.

Habitat

Adult crane flies are found in low vegetation, usually near water. The larvae of crane flies are found in fresh water or wet soil.

Diet and Feeding

Some species of crane flies are thought to feed on nectar, while other species may not feed at all as adults.

The larvae of crane flies usually feed on dead plants, but sometimes eat live plants. The larvae of some species in the Arctic can even be predators.

Life Cycle

Crane flies experience complete metamorphosis.

1. Crane flies lay up to 300 eggs in water or wet soil. Their eggs hatch after two weeks.
2. The larvae usually live in water and can burrow into wet soil or stay underwater during the winter.
3. Crane flies usually spend 5 to 12 days as pupae and can survive the winter as pupae as well.
4. Pupae hatch into flying adults. Adults can live for several days. They usually only live long enough to mate and produce young.

While in their larval stage, crane flies usually wait for good conditions in summer to complete their life cycle. In Nunavut, the full life cycle of crane flies can take up to five years as they wait for these conditions.

Did you know?

In the Arctic, crane flies are an important source of food for birds such as sandpipers.

Behaviour

You can usually tell if a crane fly is male or female by the way it flies. Females fly straight and steady, while males fly up and down.

Since crane flies look like mosquitoes, you might think they bite, but they are harmless to humans.

Traditional Knowledge

In Clyde River, Iglulik, and Iqaluit, crane flies are called *tuktuujaq* because they have long legs like caribou. *Tuktu* is the Inuktitut word for caribou.

Young boys were asked to rub crane flies on their cheeks so they would be able to catch caribou when they grew up.

HOUSEFLY

Found
all over
Nunavut

Appearance

Adult houseflies are between 0.3 and 1.2 centimetres long. Their bodies can be black, grey, or yellow. Some species of houseflies are shiny blue or green.

Houseflies have large eyes that face forward. Their antennae are short and look like feathers. Some houseflies have mouths that are like sponges that can soak up liquids. Others have sharp mouths for biting.

Houseflies have one pair of wings.

Range

Houseflies can be found all over Nunavut, including in the High and Low Arctic.

Habitat

Different species of houseflies live in different habitats, depending on what they eat. They can be found on the tundra near fresh water, dead animals or plants, fruit, or flowers. They are also often found near communities in Nunavut, since there is access to food there.

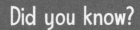

Adult houseflies are usually found in the same habitat as their larvae. This is because adults need to find areas with food for their young.

Diet and Feeding

Houseflies eat a variety of food, depending on the species. They can eat dung, pollen from plants, nectar from flowers, or dead plants. Some houseflies even hunt and eat other insects, while others feed on blood and other fluids from dead animals.

Life Cycle

Houseflies undergo complete metamorphosis.

1. Female houseflies lay their eggs where the larvae can easily find food. They can lay their eggs near dung from animals or dead animals or plants, depending on the species. Females can lay up to 500 eggs.

2. The eggs hatch into larvae.

3. The larvae become surrounded in a hardened case as they turn into pupae.

4. The pupae later become flying adults. Adults can live anywhere from 15 to 25 days.

Behaviour

Houseflies are important for pollinating plants in the High Arctic. If you are in the High Arctic and see lots of flowers, you will know there might be houseflies around.

Did you know?

Since houseflies can be found on dung and dead animals, they can cause illness in humans, such as food poisoning if they land on food that people eat.

CARIBOU WARBLE FLY

Appearance

Adult caribou warble flies are large flies that can be up to 2.5 centimetres long. Caribou warble flies have stocky, hairy bodies. They can sometimes look like bees.

The heads of caribou warble flies are wide with a flat face. They have small eyes that face forward. They also have short antennae, and their mouths are not well developed.

Adult caribou warble flies have round abdomens. They have one set of wings. They also have short, hairy legs.

**Found
all over
Nunavut**

Range

Caribou warble flies are usually found near caribou in the Low Arctic. Warble flies have been found in the High Arctic around Peary caribou.

Habitat

The habitat of caribou warble flies is wherever caribou are found.

The larvae of warble flies are found under the skin or in the noses and throats of caribou.

Diet and Feeding

Adult caribou warble flies do not feed. Instead, they survive on fat stored in their bodies from earlier life stages.

Unlike most fly larvae, the larvae of caribou warble flies are **parasites**. The larvae feed on the bodies of living animals. Caribou are important for Inuit as a food source, but they are also important for caribou warble flies. The larvae of caribou warble flies feed on blood and other fluids from the bodies of caribou.

Life Cycle

Caribou warble flies go through complete metamorphosis.

1. In summer, female caribou warble flies lay their eggs on the hair of caribou on the lower part of their bodies. The hair of the caribou protects the eggs.
2. When the eggs hatch, the larvae burrow into the skin of the caribou. The larvae travel under the skin of the caribou to the caribou's back. Once the larvae reach the caribou's back, they create tiny holes in the skin of the caribou to breathe. The larvae live in cases called warbles under the skin of the caribou through the autumn and winter. The warbles are made by the caribou's body to stop the larvae from moving. The larvae develop within the warbles.
3. In early summer, the larvae break through the skin of the caribou and drop to the ground. The larvae turn into pupae on the ground.
4. Pupae hatch into flying adults. The adults of caribou warble flies live for three to five days. Adults need to search for a mate soon after they hatch from pupae.

Behaviour

Adult male caribou warble flies gather near dry streams on rocks or plants to wait for females to mate. Once females have mated, they search for caribou by detecting the carbon dioxide that the caribou breathe out.

Traditional Knowledge

Inuit in some areas have used the larvae of warble flies as a food source, as it can be a good source of protein and nutrients.

AMERICAN COPPER BUTTERFLY

Appearance

Adult American coppers are small butterflies. They have a wingspan of about 2.5 centimetres.

The outside of the upper part of their wings is bright copper in colour, with a grey border and black spots. The outside of the bottom part of their wings is greyish-brown with a copper-coloured border.

American coppers have antennae that are ringed with a white colour. They also have white around their eyes.

Found all over Nunavut

Range

American coppers can be found all over Nunavut. They can even be found in the High Arctic, on Ellesmere Island.

Did you know?

You can tell male and female American coppers apart by their front legs. Male American coppers have smaller front legs than females. Females also have claws on their front legs, but males do not.

Habitat

American coppers are found on the tundra. They can be found on piles of rocks at the base of hills or near the plants they feed on.

Diet and Feeding

Adult American coppers feed on nectar from flowers.

The caterpillars of American coppers also eat plants. American copper caterpillars feed on mountain sorrel. They chew holes in the leaves.

Life Cycle

American coppers go through complete metamorphosis.

1. Female American coppers lay their eggs on or near the petals, stems, or undersides of plant leaves. This provides food for the caterpillars once they hatch.
2. Caterpillars are the larvae of American coppers. They move along the ground eating leaves.
3. The caterpillars turn into pupae called a chrysalis, where they develop into adults in a hardened case.
4. Adult American coppers emerge from the chrysalis. They can fly as soon as they emerge.

Behaviour

American coppers are fast fliers compared to many butterflies. They usually fly close to the ground to stay out of the wind. American coppers cannot fly until their bodies are warm. They warm their bodies by basking with their wings in the sun. If it's too cold, they may not fly for several weeks.

Adult male American coppers fly around looking for females. Males will also defend their territories and chase rival butterflies away.

BRUSH-FOOTED BUTTERFLY

Appearance

Most species of brush-footed butterflies are 4 to 6 centimetres long.

Most brush-footed butterflies are orange. The underside of the wings have dull colours. These dull colours can help with **camouflage**.

Brush-footed butterflies have short front legs that are covered in hair. Their front legs look like brushes.

Found
all over
Nunavut

Range

Different species of brush-footed butterflies can be found in both the Low and High Arctic.

Habitat

Brush-footed butterflies are found on the tundra. Some species are found in grassier areas, while others can be found in dry or wet areas.

Diet and Feeding

Adult brush-footed butterflies feed on nectar from flowers. Some species also feed on rotting fruit.

The caterpillars of brush-footed butterflies feed on different plants, depending on the species. Caterpillars eat shrubs, willow and dwarf birch plants, and grasses.

Life Cycle

All types of brush-footed butterflies found in Nunavut undergo complete metamorphosis.

1. Female brush-footed butterflies lay their eggs differently, depending on the species. They might lay their eggs near plants, on the stems of plants, on the undersides of leaves, or in clumps on willow and dwarf birch plants.

2. The caterpillars (the larvae) of brush-footed butterflies emerge from their eggs and begin to eat their favourite plants. Caterpillars may live for more than a year before turning into butterflies. Caterpillars can shed their exoskeletons several times.

3. The caterpillars turn into a chrysalis (the pupae).

4. Adult butterflies emerge from their chrysalis in the spring. Some butterflies develop more quickly and hibernate as mature caterpillars over winter.

Did you know?

Arctic brush-footed butterflies can survive in the extreme cold of Nunavut by freezing solid. These butterflies thaw in spring and continue their life cycle.

Behaviour

Adult brush-footed butterflies walk on their middle and back legs. They walk this way because their front legs are too short to walk on.

ARCTIC WOOLLY BEAR MOTH

Appearance

Adult Arctic woolly bear moths have a wingspan between 2 and 7 centimetres. Their bodies are stocky and hairy.

Adult male moths have antennae that look like feathers.

Adult male woolly bear moths have large wings, while adult females can have small wings or no wings at all.

Arctic woolly bear caterpillars (the larvae) are large and covered in dense hair. They also have a tuft of hair on their head and at the end of their abdomen. The caterpillars have slim bodies under their hair.

Range

The Arctic woolly bear moth is found in the High Arctic. They can be found on Ellesmere Island in Nunavut.

Arctic woolly bear moths can also be found in Greenland.

Habitat

Arctic woolly bear moths are found on the tundra, usually near their food.

Arctic woolly bear caterpillars are often found attached to rocks instead of plants during the winter. The caterpillars are likely found on rocks because snow on rocks thaws quickly in the spring. This would allow the caterpillars to begin to move as soon as plants are out and ready to eat.

Diet and Feeding

Arctic woolly bear moths do not eat as adults.

Arctic woolly bear caterpillars feed during the month of June. They likely feed during this time because the nutrients in their favourite food, Arctic willow, are highest in June.

Life Cycle

Arctic woolly bear moths undergo complete metamorphosis.

1. Female Arctic woolly bear moths lay their eggs in clumps on or near the **cocoon** they have emerged from.
2. When the eggs hatch into caterpillars, they shed their exoskeleton very slowly, sometimes only once per year.
3. The pupae of Arctic woolly bear moths develop inside cocoons made out of silk.
4. The adults that emerge from cocoons sometimes live for only one day.

The entire life cycle of Arctic woolly bear moths can be up to seven years long from the time they are an egg to when they become an adult. This is the longest life cycle of any butterfly or moth. Most of this time is spent as a caterpillar.

Behaviour

Arctic woolly bear caterpillars move very slowly. Their top speed is 0.08 kilometres per hour. A snowmobile can go almost 1000 times faster than an Arctic woolly bear caterpillar!

Arctic woolly bear caterpillars spend most of their time basking in the sun or feeding. They need to take advantage of the short summers in the High Arctic.

Arctic woolly bear caterpillars become inactive in winter. They can spend a lot of their lives inactive and frozen.

Did you know?

Arctic woolly bear moths are adapted to survive in temperatures below minus 60 degrees Celsius. They produce chemicals in their bodies that prevent their bodies from being damaged by freezing.

NORTHERN BUMBLE BEE

Appearance

Adult northern bumble bees are some of the larger bees found in the Canadian Arctic. The queen bees, which are 1.8 to 2.2 centimetres long, are the largest. Worker bees, which are female, are 1 to 1.6 centimetres long. Males are 1.4 to 1.6 centimetres long.

The heads of northern bumble bees have two long, straight antennae that are segmented. Their tongues are long. When they are not using their tongue, they fold it back into their head.

Northern bumble bees have two pairs of wings. Their front wings are larger than their back wings.

Female bumble bees have a stinger at the end of their abdomens.

Found
all over
Nunavut

Range

Northern bumble bees can be found all over Nunavut, including Ellesmere Island in the High Arctic.

Habitat

Adult northern bumble bees can be found on the tundra. They are found on and around flowers.

The nests of northern bumble bees are underground. Sometimes their nests are in abandoned lemming holes or patches of grass. Larvae can be found in the nests.

Diet and Feeding

Northern bumble bees feed on the nectar of the flowers of willow, blueberry, and cranberry plants. They use their long tongues to reach nectar in the flowers. Their tongues are also hairy at the end to help suck up nectar.

Life Cycle

Northern bumble bees undergo complete metamorphosis.

1. In early spring, queen bees emerge with eggs to start a new colony. Queen bees lay eggs in large groups in a new nest.

2. In summer, queen bees lay their first batch of eggs that develop into larvae, pupae, and eventually adult worker bees. Worker bees are small females that cannot breed. Worker bees make the nest bigger, find food, and take care of young bees.

3. In late summer, queen bees lay a second batch of eggs that includes male bees called drones. The second batch of eggs also includes many females that may become queens the next year.

4. In autumn, new males from other colonies mate with females produced in the second batch of eggs. All of these males and most of the females will die after reproducing. Usually only one new queen is produced that will survive the winter and start a new colony the next year. The old queen also dies off in the autumn.

The entire life cycle of queen northern bumble bees occurs within one year.

Behaviour

Northern bumble bees in the High Arctic use their flight muscles to keep themselves warm by shivering. Then, the hair on the bees traps this heat and keeps them warm.

Did you know?

Northern bumble bees may be threatened by **climate change**, because they are adapted to the Arctic. Climate change may bring future changes to plants and other insects found in the habitat of bees in the Arctic.

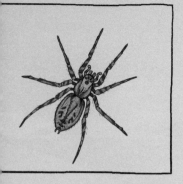

WOLF SPIDER

Found
all over
Nunavut

Appearance

Wolf spiders are large spiders. They can be up to 4 centimetres long. Female wolf spiders are larger than males.

The bodies of wolf spiders are divided into two round sections. The exoskeleton of wolf spiders is dark in colour and can have dark bands that help with camouflage.

Wolf spiders have eight eyes in three rows. The first row has four small eyes in a straight line. The second row has two larger eyes that look forward. The third row has two more large eyes that look up.

Spiders have eight legs. This makes them different from insects, which have six legs.

Range

Wolf spiders can be found all over Nunavut. Some species are found in the High Arctic.

Habitat

Wolf spiders can be found on the tundra. They live under rocks or out in the open. Some wolf spiders dig holes for shelter.

Diet and Feeding

Wolf spiders are **carnivores**. They hunt and eat insects they find on the ground.

Adult wolf spiders can even eat young wolf spiders. This means they are **cannibals**.

Life Cycle

Wolf spiders are not insects, so their life cycle is different from the insect species in this book.

Female wolf spiders lay several dozen eggs. They spin a round egg sac to carry their eggs. Females carry the egg sac at the back of their bodies.

Young spiders are called spiderlings. When spiderlings hatch from eggs, they are carried around on their mother's abdomen by hanging on to specialized hairs. Spiderlings do not eat while they are on their mother's body. Female spiders care for their spiderlings.

Male wolf spiders usually live for one year, while females can live up to three years.

Behaviour

Wolf spiders usually hide and wait for their insect prey.

Unlike many spiders, most species of wolf spider do not spin webs.

Wolf spiders are mostly found by themselves. They come together to mate. Males put on a display for females during mating.

Did you know?

With climate change, spring is arriving earlier in the Arctic. This helps wolf spiders in the High Arctic produce more young. Wolf spiders in the High Arctic are sometimes able to produce two sets of eggs instead of one. Spiders in the south usually produce multiple sets of eggs each year.

GLOSSARY

algae: tiny plant-like organisms found in water.

arachnid: a type of animal that has a segmented body, an exoskeleton, and limbs. Spiders, scorpions, ticks, and mites are arachnids.

camouflage: appearance that helps objects blend in with their environment; for example, the grey colour of some insects may help them blend in with rocks.

cannibal: an organism that eats members of its own species—for example, wolf spiders that eat their young.

carnivore: an organism that eats meat.

caterpillar: the larva of a butterfly or moth.

climate change: a shift in weather patterns over a long period of time—for example, a change in temperature patterns in the springtime in the High Arctic.

cocoon: a case made out of silk that contains the pupae of moths.

ecosystem: a community of all the living things, such as insects and animals, and their environment in an area.

evolve: to change slowly. For insects and other animals, evolution takes millions of years.

exoskeleton: the hard outer part of an insect's body.

larva (plural larvae): an early stage in the life of insects that hatch from eggs. Larvae of insects do not look like the adults.

metamorphosis: the change from one form to a completely different form.

molting: shedding old feathers, hair, skin, a shell, or an exoskeleton to make way for new growth.

nectar: a sugary liquid produced by plants, usually by flowers.

parasite: an organism that lives on another organism (called the host organism). Parasites harm the host organism they live on as they get their food from the host organism.

pollinate: the transfer of pollen from different parts of plants to allow them to reproduce.

predator: an organism that eats and kills other organisms.

pupa (plural pupae): an early stage in the life of an insect in between the larval and adult life stages.

scavenger: an organism that feeds on dead organisms.

segmented: formed of a series of similar parts.

standing water: water without waves or movement—for example, a small puddle.

INHABIT
EDUCATION
BOOKS